History in Evidence

TUDOR BRITAIN

Tony D. Triggs

History in Evidence

Medieval Britain

Norman Britain

Prehistoric Britain

Roman Britain

Saxon Britain

Tudor Britain

Victorian Britain

Viking Britain

Cover design: Alison Anholt-White
Series design: Helen White
Consultant: Dr Margaret L Faull

Cover pictures: The main picture shows Little Moreton Hall, in Cheshire. The inset is a painting on glass in a window of Oxburgh Hall, Norfolk.

First published in 1989 by
Wayland (Publishers) Limited
61 Western Road, Hove
East Sussex BN3 1JD, England

Second impression 1991

British Library Cataloguing in Publication Data
Triggs, Tony D.
    Tudor Britain.
    1. Great Britain, 1485–1603
    I. Title   II. Series
    941.05

HARDBACK ISBN 1-85210-581-X

PAPERBACK ISBN 0-7502-0545-8

Edited and typeset by Kudos, Hove, East Sussex
Printed in Italy by G. Canale & C.Sp.A., Turin
Bound in France by A.G.M.

Picture acknowledgements
The publishers wish to thank the following for permission to reproduce their illustrations on the pages mentioned: Chapel Studios Picture Library 7 (lower), 25 (lower); C M Dixon/Photoresources 6, 29 (upper); ET Archive 15; Hulton Picture Library 24; Kudos 28; National Trust *cover* (both), 7 (upper), 8, 10, 11 (upper), 19 (lower), 23 (upper); Ronald Sheridan/Ancient Art & Architecture Collection 11 (lower), 27; *Mary Rose* Trust 16, 18, 22, 23 (lower), 29 (lower); Skyscan 5 (© Kentwell Hall), 13, 20, 21 (both); TOPHAM 9 (both), 14, 25 (top), 26; Weald & Downland Open Air Museum 12; Stephen White-Thomson 17. The pictures on pages 4 and 19 (upper) came from the Wayland Picture Library. The artwork on page 4 was supplied by Malcolm S Walker.

Contents

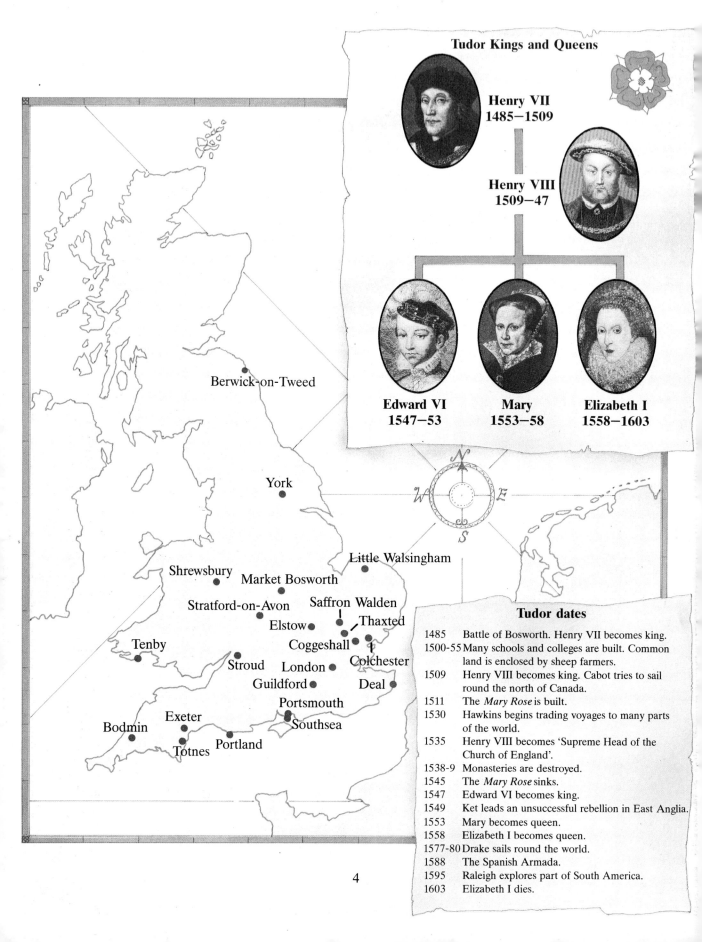

Tudor Kings and Queens

Henry VII
1485—1509

Henry VIII
1509—47

Edward VI
1547—53

Mary
1553—58

Elizabeth I
1558—1603

Berwick-on-Tweed

York

Little Walsingham

Shrewsbury

Market Bosworth

Stratford-on-Avon

Saffron Walden

Elstow

Thaxted

Coggeshall

Colchester

Tenby

Stroud

London

Deal

Guildford

Portsmouth

Bodmin

Exeter

Southsea

Totnes

Portland

Tudor dates

1485	Battle of Bosworth. Henry VII becomes king.
1500-55	Many schools and colleges are built. Common land is enclosed by sheep farmers.
1509	Henry VIII becomes king. Cabot tries to sail round the north of Canada.
1511	The *Mary Rose* is built.
1530	Hawkins begins trading voyages to many parts of the world.
1535	Henry VIII becomes 'Supreme Head of the Church of England'.
1538-9	Monasteries are destroyed.
1545	The *Mary Rose* sinks.
1547	Edward VI becomes king.
1549	Ket leads an unsuccessful rebellion in East Anglia.
1553	Mary becomes queen.
1558	Elizabeth I becomes queen.
1577-80	Drake sails round the world.
1588	The Spanish Armada.
1595	Raleigh explores part of South America.
1603	Elizabeth I dies.

Who were the Tudors?

ABOVE The courtyard of Kentwell Hall, in Suffolk, with its stone pattern in the shape of a Tudor rose.

OPPOSITE All the places mentioned in this book are shown on this map, as well as the main towns of Tudor Britain. There is also a list of important dates and a family tree of the Tudor kings and queens.

The Tudors were the kings and queens who ruled England and Wales from 1485 to 1603. Until 1485 two branches of the royal family had fought each other for the throne. The branches are known as the House of Lancaster and the House of York, and the wars between them are usually known as the Wars of the Roses, since each side had a rose on its badge.

The final battle of the Wars took place near Market Bosworth in Leicestershire, and is usually known as the Battle of Bosworth. It was fought in 1485, and the armies were led by King Richard III, from the House of York, and Henry Tudor, who belonged to the House of Lancaster. Richard was killed, and Henry became King Henry VII – the first of the Tudors. He took a number of steps which ended the Wars for good: for example, he married Princess Elizabeth from the House of York, and this encouraged friendly relations between the two branches of the royal family.

Henry and Elizabeth had two sons, and one became king when Henry died. He was Henry VIII, and he reigned from 1509 to 1547. He was followed by his son Edward VI and then by his daughters Mary and Elizabeth. Elizabeth did not have any children, so when she died in 1603, the line of the Tudor kings and queens came to an end. In this book we will look at life under the Tudors.

Town life

Drawn in 1587, this map of Exeter gives us an idea of what a Tudor town looked like. Although the map shows wide streets and open spaces, people lived in cramped and unhealthy conditions.

In Tudor times most towns were very small indeed, often with only a few hundred houses. Many towns had walls around them to keep out attackers. Most of the walls were very old, but Berwick-on-Tweed had walls that were built by the Tudor people themselves.

In the towns the Tudors made and traded things, so goods and supplies were arriving and leaving all the time. Most of these were carried in horse-drawn wagons. In winter the wagons often got stuck when the roads became muddy. Since most towns stood on river banks, boats were also important for carrying goods, and rivers provided power for corn mills and other machinery.

All Tudor towns were cramped and

unhealthy, and craftsmen and traders filled the streets with noise and filth. People ate more fish and meat than they do today, and many towns, like York, had streets or districts known as the Shambles. Shambles were the benches butchers used for killing cattle and chopping up and selling meat. Sometimes, butchers worked in the street outside their houses, but most of

ABOVE Here is the front of a typical Tudor town house. This one faces a street in Paycockes, in Essex.

We are surrounded by evidence of Tudor Britain. These shops along a street in Shrewsbury have changed little since they were built in the 1500s.

them used their downstairs rooms as shops.

Besides its Shambles, a town might have a Pudding Lane, a Fish Street, a Shoemakers' Street and other streets where particular trades were carried out. Few people could read, so traders used signs to show what sort of work they did. Barbers sometimes displayed a sign called a barber's pole, and examples can still be seen today. The red and white spiral reminds us that barbers used to practise simple medicine, like pulling out teeth and removing warts. The red stands for blood and the white stands for healthy skin or bandages.

Business is booming!

Many of the traders in Tudor towns had young apprentices (assistants who were learning the trade). Apprentices (mainly boys) had to live with traders and work without pay. We know about their lives from documents, called 'Apprentice Rolls', which have survived. An apprenticeship lasted seven years, and then the young man could work as a journeyman (someone who was paid for each day's work he did).

Later he could set up shop and even

Many Tudors became wealthy through trade, so they could afford beautiful furniture and well-built houses. This is the dining-room of a rich merchant's house in Tenby, Dyfed.

LEFT As trade grew, so the guilds became more powerful. They would meet in halls like this one in Thaxted, Essex.

have his own apprentices. If he did set up shop, he would have to pay to join a guild. There were various guilds, and each looked after the people who did a particular job. The guilds made sure that outsiders could not come into the town and take away their members' trade.

Each guild had a meeting place, or 'guildhall'. The finest guildhall often belonged to the wealthy merchants who sent goods abroad. Sometimes their guildhall was used for running the town's affairs. A few Tudor guildhalls are still in use as town halls today (see page 30). We can also see Tudor merchants' houses in some modern towns (see page 30). They were bigger and finer than most other houses built by the Tudors.

Documents have survived to show that overseas trade was very important in Tudor times. Cloth was shipped to Europe, and ivory, spices, silk and gold were imported. Most of these goods came from Asia, and explorers tried to find new ways to get there. They tried to sail round the north of Canada and also Russia. Both routes were blocked by frozen seas, but the explorers found new people to trade with. By the end of the 1500s, Tudor merchants were buying furs and timber from Russia and other countries around the Baltic Sea.

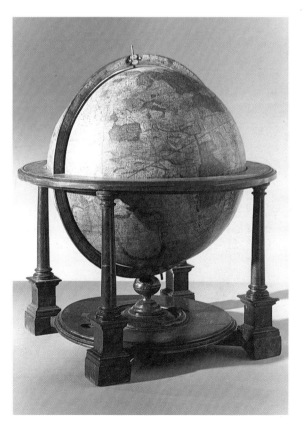

LEFT This globe was made in 1541. It was used by a sea captain on his voyages.

Mansions

One of the main bedrooms at Oxburgh Hall, in Norfolk. The huge fire, where logs were burnt, helped to keep it warm in winter.

Many of the richest Tudors lived in mansions in the country. Up to this time, the wealthy had often built fortified homes, with towers and thick walls. However, gunpowder had been introduced in the 1400s, and it was hard to make houses safe from bombs and cannon balls. The Tudors therefore gave up trying to make their houses as strong as possible; instead, they tried to make them grand and comfortable. They tried all sorts of layouts and styles, and their houses often had many windows. Earlier buildings had avoided big windows because glass was expensive and the windows would have let in attackers. However, glass was now cheaper, so the rich Tudors, especially, used a lot of it in their houses.

The main downstairs room was the dining-hall. It was long and narrow, with a platform at one end where the owner and his family sat and dined. Guests' tables ran down each side of the hall, and the poorest or least important guests sat near the door which led to the kitchens and the servants' rooms. A door at the opposite end of the hall led from the owner's table to his private rooms. Most of the upstairs part of the house consisted of bedrooms and rooms for guests. They were comfortably furnished, and, unlike town houses, some mansions even had running water and proper toilets.

Tudor mansions were often huge, with up to 150 servants. The servants had all sorts of chores, besides preparing food and drink. For example, they had to look after the blazing coal-fires which kept the mansion warm. Earlier homes had been poorly heated, often with only a single fire and draughty holes to let the smoke out. Most Tudor mansions had chimneys, so lots of fires could be burned without any trouble from smoke or draughts.

ABOVE The main hall of Cotehele House, in Cornwall, with armour from the 1500s.

Tudor mansions often had many windows because glass had become cheaper. This is the front of Hardwick Hall, in Derbyshire.

Country life

Most Tudor mansions were 'manor houses'. In other words, the family owned the surrounding land, which might include a village with up to 1,000 people. Most of the villagers grew their own crops on separate strips of land near their homes. They also kept some sheep and cattle on land which they shared (called 'common land'). Their animals gave them milk, meat, and wool which they could spin and weave to make themselves clothes. The villagers had to pay the owner (or 'lord') of the manor for using his land. Some paid in cash; others paid by giving the lord a share of their produce or doing some work for him.

These were difficult times for the village folk. Many lords of the manor began to rear huge flocks of sheep, which provided the wool for England's trade in

At the Weald and Downland Open Air Museum in West Sussex, you can see buildings from many periods in British history. This is a copy of a typical Tudor farmhouse at the museum.

A Tudor farmhouse at Deerhurst in the heart of the Gloucestershire countryside.

cloth. Soon they began to fence in the common land for their flocks, and this made it hard for the villagers to feed their own animals. As a result, they began to go short of food and clothes. Some started earning money as shepherds, but others became extremely poor. Often they were forced to go begging in nearby towns, though the citizens tried to keep them out. The lords of the manor were usually glad to see them go. They pulled down the villagers' tiny homes and turned their strips of farmland into extra grazing for their sheep. There are many parts of England where we can see the remains of villages which the Tudors abandoned.

The 'Mary Rose'

A special steel cradle was built to raise the *Mary Rose*'s hull to the surface. A gigantic crane lifted the cradle out of the water on 11 October 1982.

The *Mary Rose* was a Tudor warship. Henry VIII had it built soon after he came to the throne, but it suddenly sank as it sailed out of Portsmouth Harbour in 1545. The sides of the ship had special holes for its giant guns, and some of the holes may have been too low. Maybe a gust of wind caught the ship and tilted it over, allowing water to gush in and sink it.

The *Mary Rose* lay hidden for over 400 hundred years. No one could see it from the surface because the water was muddy, and a layer of mud sometimes hid it from divers. In the 1970s, a group of archaeologists decided to explore it, but first they had to find exactly where it was. They used sonar equipment to help in their search. Sonar works by sending sound waves through the water and picking them up when they bounce off objects. When the sonar detected something in the mud, the archaeologists had to find out what it was, so they disappeared over the side of their boat in diving suits!

Once they had found the *Mary Rose*, they studied it using video cameras and other scientific equipment. Much of the ship had rotted away, but many cabins could still be explored. The filthy water made the job extremely hard, and the workers had to use suction tubes to get rid of mud. They carefully saved all the Tudor objects they could find, and they also saved any parts of the ship which they had to remove. This was because they planned to get the hull on to land and then put back the parts they had saved.

At last, on 11 October 1982, the hull of the ship was lifted out of the water with a giant crane. It is very weak and it has to be sprayed with very cold water to stop it drying out and crumbling to pieces. It is now on display in a special museum at Portsmouth, and visitors can also see some of the 14,000 objects which were found in the ship. They show us what life was like for sailors in Tudor times, and they also give us clues about Tudor life on land.

A page from the 'Anthony Roll' of 1546 showing the *Mary Rose*. The Roll was a list of all Henry VIII's ships and their equipment.

Warfare

This magnificent bronze gun was recovered from the *Mary Rose* in 1979. The wooden gun carriage, in which it rests, was made by modern-day craftsmen.

The Tudors went to war against the French and Spanish. Their navy was large and well-equipped, and they always kept it ready for action. Thousands of arrows and 169 bows were found on board the *Mary Rose*. Some had been carefully tied in bundles and packed in chests. Others were poked through the holes in special pieces of leather. There were 24 holes, so each piece of leather bristled with arrows. This helped the archers to grab arrows quickly during a battle. Leather 'bracers' were also found on the *Mary Rose*: the archers wore them to stop their wrists being grazed by the bow-string.

The archaeologists also found a number of long-bows on the ship. Some were used to fire burning arrows or other objects at enemy vessels. Barrels of tar and cauldrons were found, so the objects were probably dipped in molten tar and then lit. Tudor ships were made of wood, and they also had lots of sails and rigging, so fires could be started easily.

Sometimes the Tudors used blazing ships to damage the enemy fleet. They were used in 1588 against the huge Spanish fleet (called the Armada) which was threatening England.

Arrows and fire were not the only weapons Tudor sailors could use. As we have seen, their ships carried cannons. Cannons were also used on land, and so were smaller guns, known as muskets. Soldiers carried muskets with them. However, they were clumsy and heavy. They always took a long time to load and the shot did not go very far. If two armies met, they had to get very close to each other before the musketeers could open fire. Arrows could travel further than bullets.

Often, the front line of soldiers had pikes (like long spears) instead of muskets. They used them to form a sloping 'fence' with the points facing towards the enemy. The fence of pikes discouraged enemy soldiers from charging, even on horseback. The pikes would have gone right through their bodies. When the battle-lines broke, there was hand-to-hand fighting. The soldiers used their muskets as clubs, and they also fought with swords, pikes and special spears, called bills, which were used for slashing and stabbing.

ABOVE Members of a modern-day Tudor army who meet regularly to re-enact Tudor battles. Their weapons and armour are copies of those used by Tudor soldiers.

Clothes

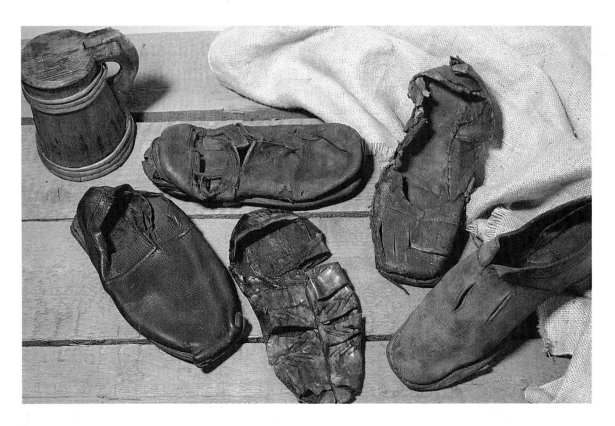

These leather shoes were once worn by soldiers and sailors on board the *Mary Rose*. They were preserved in the mud at the bottom of Portsmouth Harbour.

Many Tudor clothes have survived to the present day. (Some were even found on board the *Mary Rose*.) There are several museums where these can be seen (see page 30), and they give us a very good idea of what the Tudors wore. Tudor portrait paintings also survive, but we have to remember that most of them show wealthy people in all their finery. There are pictures of Tudor kings and queens, and also famous Tudors like Sir Thomas More and Sir Walter Raleigh.

Sir Thomas More lived in the reigns of Henry VII and Henry VIII, and in those days men and women used to wrap themselves up in big loose gowns. Gowns like this were worn throughout the Tudor period, but fashions were changing. Sir Walter Raleigh lived in Queen Elizabeth's reign, and by then most well-off men and boys wore doublets and hose. Men also wore silk stockings – and sometimes

It is hard to explain every change in fashion. However, we know that the Tudors were learning to heat their homes efficiently, so the huge woollen gowns were no longer quite so important for warmth. We also know that explorers and traders were coming home with silks and all sorts of precious stones. This helps to explain why clothes for the rich were so fine and colourful.

Poorer people could not afford silk! Most women wore several layers of linen or woollen cloth with a belt round the waist. Their husbands wore plain jerkins (or jackets) made of leather. They also wore rough woollen trousers and sturdy leather boots or shoes.

ABOVE This is a painting of Lord Burghley, who was an important adviser to Queen Elizabeth. It shows us how rich people dressed in the late 1500s.

woollen ones – to keep their legs warm.

Gowns were normally made of wool and they sometimes made the wearer itch, so most people liked to wear linen garments against their skin. Most women wore kirtles (like very simple linen dresses) under their gowns. As gowns became less popular, they started to wear embroidered kirtles; then they began to wear separate garments – a bodice and a very long skirt. They sometimes made their skirts stand out with hoops made of whalebone, wire or wood, while men stuffed their breeches with padding.

This stained-glass window from Oxburgh Hall, Norfolk, shows us the clothes worn by a merchant and his wife.

Henry VIII and the Church

When Henry VII became king, England had over 600 monasteries. These were places where monks or nuns lived, prayed, worked and studied. Each monastery had a church where the monks or nuns prayed together up to eight times a day. However, there were other buildings where they slept, prepared their food and ate. Monasteries usually owned rich farmland, and this provided the monks or nuns with all they required. Their life was meant to be very simple and even harsh. In many monasteries the monks or nuns were forbidden to speak to each other; they were

Hampton Court, in London, was once the luxurious home of Cardinal Wolsey, who lived at the time of Henry VIII. Wealth from the monasteries helped to make Cardinal Wolsey very rich.

not allowed to own things or have any pleasures – except the pleasure of praying. Some monks and nuns obeyed the rules, but others lived a more comfortable life. The monasteries grew extremely rich, and some of the money went to clergy who lived in luxury. The best example was Cardinal Wolsey, who owned a palace called Hampton Court, in London.

In Henry VIII's reign, many Tudors complained about the Church and the monasteries. Some, like Sir Thomas More, simply wanted the rules to be obeyed more strictly. Others had their greedy eyes on the monasteries' land. Henry became involved because he wished to divorce his first wife, Catherine, and marry Anne Boleyn. In those days England belonged to the Roman Catholic Church, and its head was the Pope, who lived in Rome. The divorce really needed the Pope's permission, but Henry arranged his own divorce. He also declared that he

Tintern Abbey, in Gwent – one of the monasteries destroyed by Henry VIII.

was the head of the Church in England. He executed a number of monks who spoke against him; then he closed the monasteries and had nearly all the buildings pulled down. This stopped monks and nuns from opposing him and it also meant that Henry could share the monasteries' wealth and land with his followers.

The remains of many monasteries can still be seen. In a few cases, monastery churches were turned into churches for local people to pray in, and these are in use today. In most cases, only the ruins remain, including the ruins of dormitories, kitchens and other rooms. There are fine examples in Yorkshire and Norfolk, and they show us a lot about monastery life. For example, we can easily see why monasteries were built near rivers. The river provided drinking water and saved the monks and nuns from having to bury the filth from their toilets (the toilets were usually built directly above the stream).

Rievaulx Abbey, North Yorkshire, was also ruined on Henry VIII's orders.

Good food and bad

ABOVE These two cooking pots, made out of copper, were found by some divers near the galley (kitchen) in the *Mary Rose*'s hull.

Foreigners were often amazed at how much the Tudors ate. Perhaps they stayed with well-off people and not the poor, for they told of feasts with course after course of venison and other meats. One course often consisted of birds, such as blackbirds and larks.

Only the rich could hunt or buy such a wide range of meats. The poor ate very little meat. Their main food was bread, and they sometimes caught rabbits, hares and fish. They also ate turnips, beans and cabbage. They sometimes made themselves vegetable soup and added pieces of bread to the mixture.

Few Tudors ever saw potatoes. They were brought to Britain by explorers, such as Sir Walter Raleigh. Raleigh made his voyages in the reign of Queen Elizabeth, the last of the Tudor kings and queens. Potatoes were far too heavy to bring to Britain in bulk, and very few farmers tried to grow them.

Sugar was also very scarce in Tudor times, but when they obtained it, the Tudors used it on most of their food, including meat. Their other way of sweetening food was to add some honey.

The Tudors were very keen on spices. This was partly because they salted their meat to stop it going off. Spices helped to hide the taste of the salt; they also hid the unpleasant taste of bad meat!

Many Tudors ate too much salt and not enough vegetables. This was especially true of sailors, who often had to live for months on salted meat, hard biscuits and beer, with a little fish if they could catch it. The sailors' bad diet often gave them an illness called scurvy. Their gums began to rot away and their breath became foul. We know this because ships' captains wrote reports about voyages. We also know this because bodies were found on the *Mary Rose*. The sailors had drowned, but some were already dying of scurvy; one was losing his teeth because his gums were in such a terrible state.

People who went to Tudor theatres were fed quite well! During performances, food and drink were carried round the audience, and many Tudor letters and diaries mention the noise of nuts being cracked, eaten or trodden on!

ABOVE Much of the food was cooked on this fire in Cotehele House, Cornwall.

These pewter dishes, spoons and tankard were used at meal times by sailors on board the *Mary Rose*.

Going to school

Most village children never went to school in their lives, but a few attended a local 'dame school'. The dame school was run by a woman who taught her pupils the letters of the alphabet and helped the cleverer ones to read. Dame schools rarely had proper books, but a few had 'horn books'. A horn book consisted of a piece of wood in the shape of a table-tennis bat. On one side there was a printed page, held down and protected by a glass-like sheet of animal's horn. The page showed the alphabet and perhaps some simple words or a prayer.

Children from better-off families might have some books or horn books at home. They might even have a tutor to teach them reading, French and other subjects, and the boys were usually sent to school from the age of 8. They went to proper schools, not dame schools, and many boys had a long way to travel. They might have

Pictures have survived from Tudor times which tell us about daily life then. This one shows what a Tudor classroom was like during a lesson.

ABOVE This courtyard of Trinity College, in Cambridge, was built in Tudor times.

schools were forced to close down, but Parliament paid to keep some of them going, and Parliament, guilds and wealthy merchants started some new ones. Others were started under Edward VI, and several towns have schools named after him. In many cases, the Tudor buildings no longer exist, but they can still be seen at Guildford and Shrewsbury.

Life for the pupils was very hard. Lessons went from dawn until dusk, with a break for school lunch. (This might consist of ryebread, salted meat and ale.) The schoolmaster frequently beat his pupils, and he might have to teach an entire school of 60 boys in one classroom.

The pupils wrote with a quill pen, and it often had to be sharpened with a knife. The word 'penknife' reminds us that sharpening pens was a daily chore in Tudor schools.

to spend several hours a day walking to and from school, and some had to live in the schoolmaster's house.

At the start of the Tudor period, most schools belonged to monasteries, where the boys were taught the things they would need to know as monks or priests. The main subject was Latin, since many books were in Latin and it was also used for church services. Most boys left without becoming monks or priests and their education helped them in other jobs, like the law.

Under Henry VIII most monastery

This grammar school in Shrewsbury, Shropshire, was built in Henry VIII's reign after he had closed many monastery schools.

Medicine

In Tudor times few people lived to be older than 40, and many died before they were 5. This was largely because diseases thrived in the filthy, overcrowded towns. The cobbled streets were usually littered with refuse and dung. Open sewers carried some of the filth to the nearest stream, but the streets must have buzzed with flies in the summer.

At Bodmin, in Cornwall, one street had its kitchens and stables built on the higher ground at the back, and a Tudor writer described how heavy rain washed the filth right through people's homes.

The Tudors made an effort to give their houses toilets, even if they were little more than holes in the ground outside the back door. They also built public pumps and wells so that people could go and get themselves water. However, the water was rarely clean. It came from the nearest stream or river, and filth from the town had usually made it unfit to drink.

When people fell ill, they often used medicines made from plants. Country people grew their own herbs and made their own medicines, but townspeople usually bought them from an apothecary (a herbalist).

As we have seen, there were also barbers who carried out simple operations. 'Letting' (releasing) blood was very common, since people believed that having too much blood in their bodies caused

ABOVE Some of the equipment used by the barber-surgeon on board the *Mary Rose*. As well as cutting hair, he also supplied medicines for illnesses and operated on wounds.

all sorts of illnesses. Sometimes the barber made a deep cut in the patient's flesh and the blood flowed out freely. At other times he made a scratch and then used a heated cup to suck out a few drops of blood. People could also use leeches to suck out some of their blood.

Diseases in Tudor Britain included malaria, typhus and the plague. Nowadays we know that they are not caused by having too much blood. Malaria is spread by mosquitoes; typhus is spread by dirty water and the plague is spread by rats. All these dangers to health were common in Tudor towns.

This is a picture from the 1500s which shows the inside of a hospital. At the bottom, two nurses are preparing a dead patient for burial.

Pastimes

People were angry when builders wanted to put up offices on top of the remains of the Rose Theatre, in Southwark, London, where two of Shakespeare's plays were first performed.

Some of the Tudors' pastimes helped them to practise skills they would need in war. Bows and arrows were used in battle, and most Tudor men were skilful archers. Villagers set up targets to aim at; the wealthy went hunting, using bows and arrows to kill deer and wild boar, which they ate at their feasts.

Rich people often avoided taking part in wars; they usually sent the poor to fight for them, but they still based a lot of their pastimes on war. For example, they had jousting or tilting contests in which they used lances to knock each other off their horses. Rich people were also keen on fencing and they sometimes killed each other in duels.

Poor people liked to watch animal baiting. A Tudor writer called John Stow said that in Southwark (part of London) there were: *two bear gardens with bears, bulls and other beasts to be baited* [by savage dogs] ... *in a plot of ground* [fenced in] *for the beholders to stand safe.*

Other public shows were given by wandering actors. Some went in groups from inn to inn, performing in courtyards while people crowded at windows to watch. Proper theatres were built in London and they were modelled on the inns and their courtyards. We can tell this from some Tudor drawings which have survived and also from recent excavations. One of the theatres was called 'The Rose'. Its remains were uncovered in 1989. Plays by William Shakespeare were performed there in Queen Elizabeth's reign.

Rich people sometimes took part in plays (called masques) at their mansions. Masques included music and dancing.

The poor preferred outdoor activities, some of which were done at special times of the year. For example, spring was the time for pancake races and maypole

A wall painting from Queen Elizabeth's reign of a woman playing a lute.

ABOVE A folding backgammon board which was recovered from the *Mary Rose*.

dancing. They also played a rough sort of football; they chased each other from village to village, and a Tudor writer says that they often pounced on each other: 'Sometimes their necks are broken, sometimes their backs, sometimes their legs, sometimes their arms.'

In quieter moments, people played board games, bowls, and gambling games with dice, cards and dominoes, which sometimes led to quarrels.

Places to visit

Country houses
Barrington Court, Somerset
Cotehele House, Cornwall
Doddington Hall, Lincolnshire
Hampton Court, Richmond, London
Hardwick Hall, Derbyshire
Layer Marney Towers, Essex
Little Moreton Hall, Cheshire
Longleat, Wiltshire
Loseley House, Surrey
Melford Hall, Suffolk
Oxburgh Hall, Norfolk
Sherborne Castle and Sherborne Old
  Castle, Dorset

Town buildings
Coggeshall, Essex: merchant's house
Colchester, Essex: houses and inns
Elstow, Bedfordshire: moot hall
Exeter, Devon: guildhall
Little Walsingham, Norfolk: houses
Saffron Walden, Essex: houses and inns
Shrewsbury, Shropshire: various
  buildings
Stratford-on-Avon, Warwickshire:
  various buildings
Stroud, Gloucestershire: town hall and
  Shambles
Tenby, Pembrokeshire: merchant's
  house
Thaxted, Essex: houses and guildhall
Totnes, Devon: guildhall
York, Yorkshire: Shambles

Churches (and chapels inside them)
Beverley, East Yorkshire
Cirencester, Gloucestershire
Ely, Cambridgeshire
Ingatestone, Essex
Launceston, Cornwall
Lavenham, Suffolk
Oxburgh, Norfolk

Remains of monasteries
Buildwas, Shropshire
Castle Acre, Norfolk
Fountains Abbey, North Yorkshire
Jervaulx Abbey, North Yorkshire
Rievaulx Abbey, North Yorkshire
Tintern Abbey, Gwent

Fortifications
Berwick-on-Tweed, Northumberland
Deal, Kent
Portland, Dorset
Southsea, Hampshire

Almshouses
Audley End, Essex
Canterbury, Kent
Croydon, Surrey
Ledsham, West Yorkshire
Tiverton, Devon
Wirksworth, Derbyshire

Museums and exhibitions
The *Mary Rose*, Portsmouth, Hampshire

Glossary

Ale An old name for beer.

Bodice The top part of a woman's dress.

Cauldron A large metal bowl usually used for cooking.

Chore An unpleasant or boring job you have to do regularly.

Clergy The people who lead church services.

Cobbled Something that is made with smooth, round stones. It usually refers to a street which has a surface of these stones.

Cramped Squeezed into a small space.

Doublet A type of tight-fitting jacket.

Embroidered Cloth decorated with sewn patterns or pictures.

Export To sell goods to another country.

Finery Beautiful clothes and jewellery.

Fortified A place that has been protected against attack from an enemy.

Gown A long, loose piece of clothing.

Harsh Uncomfortable.

Hose Short trousers, buttoned below the knee.

Import To buy goods from another country.

Linen Cloth made from the flax plant.

Merchant A business man who buys and sells things.

Molten Runny because it is very hot.

Quill A large feather, which can be used for a pen.

Scarce Not often seen.

Books to read

Connatty, M. *The National Trust Book of the Armada* (Kingfisher, 1987)

Fines, J. *Tudor People* (Batsford, 1977)

Freeman, E. *Tudor Life and Dress* (Nelson, 1981)

Hart, R. *English Life in Tudor Times* (Wayland, 1972)

Jones, M. *Tudor and Stuart Towns* (Batsford, 1982)

Lane, P. *Tudor England* (Batsford, 1977)

Middleton, H. *Everyday Life in the Sixteenth Century* (Macdonald, 1982)

Miller, P. *Life in Elizabethan England* (Methuen, 1976)

Morrison, I. *Wreck and Rescue* [about the *Mary Rose*] (Lutterworth, 1988)

Sauvain, P. *A Tudor Mansion* (Macmillan Education, 1976)

Turner, D. *Queen Elizabeth I* (Wayland, 1987)

Unstead, R. *Life in the Elizabethan Court* (A & C Black, 1974)

Young Archaeologists Club

If you are interested in finding out more about archaeology, you might like to join this club: Young Archaeologists Club, United House, Piccadilly, York PO1 1PQ.

Index